For Richard -

His love of these great woods
has been an inspiration to
us all.

With love,

David

100 Views of the Adirondacks

FOREWORD BY MARIO CUOMO

100 Views

PHOTOGRAPHS BY NATHAN FARB

of the Adirondacks

This book is dedicated to
Peggy O'Brien (1914-1987) and Harry Eldridge (1935-1987).
They loved the Adirondacks and devoted
a tremendous amount of energy to
helping others understand, respect, and appreciate
this awesome gift of nature.

First Published in the United States of America in 1989 by
RIZZOLI INTERNATIONAL PUBLICATIONS, INC.
597 Fifth Avenue, New York, NY 10017

LC 88-43467
ISBN 0-8478-1032-1

Designed by Nai Chang
Set in type by David E. Seham Associates, Metuchen, NJ
Printed and bound in Japan by Dai Nippon Printing Co., Ltd.

Frontispiece: Sunrise from Whiteface Mountain

Mario M. Cuomo

GOVERNOR, STATE OF NEW YORK

FOREWORD

New York's Adirondacks region is one of America's great treasures. People flock from all over the United States to go hiking on its trails, to camp by its lakes, to view some of the most beautiful expanses of land and wilderness in North America.

One popular Adirondacks tale involves two tourists and a conservation officer. The tourists, smitten with the beauty of the preserve, commented on how lucky the officer was to work in such surroundings.

"Have you lived here all your life?" they asked.

He smiled and said, "Not yet I haven't."

If Nathan Farb's portfolio of photographs does not persuade you to spend the rest of your days living in the Adirondacks, I am confident it will encourage you to visit the largest and most environmentally sound wilderness area east of the Mississippi River.

The Adirondacks are especially breathtaking in autumn. Leaves, tinted orange and yellow, light up the forest from the St. Lawrence to the Mohawk Valley. At night, from the peak of Whiteface Mountain, thousands of stars, not normally visible through the pale fog of the city, beam down, offering a glimpse of eternity.

You should remember that the magnificence of the Adirondacks is ours to behold primarily because a group of New Yorkers had the foresight a century ago to take special measures to protect it. Those ecological pioneers joined together in 1895 and declared with simple eloquence that these lands be "forever wild." They wrote into law the simple truth that we could no longer hope to survive if we went on destroying the natural surroundings that support us all.

It was a significant declaration, one New York has honored and upheld. The Adirondacks are an invaluable legacy. We are proud that what was once only 680,000 acres of state-owned preservation is now a permanent living monument totaling almost two-and-a-half million acres.

Ironically, it is easier to keep the Adirondacks wild than it is to keep the wilderness safe from environmental damage. Today, the Adirondacks region is threatened by the same air and water that used to sustain it. While the potential impact of global warming, the "Greenhouse Effect," is only beginning to be understood, the droplets of acid rain are already taking their toll. Fish can no longer swim in more than 200 Adirondack lakes and ponds. Hundreds of additional lakes are endangered, costing New York billions of dollars in damage—and crippling the environment in ways only nature can fully understand.

In 1984, New York State took an important step toward reversing this trend by passing the first law in the nation to lower emissions that cause the acidity in rain. More recently, New York reached a landmark agreement with the State of Ohio that provides the framework for a national program which could reduce sulfur-dioxide emissions by more than ten-million tons over the next two decades.

Clearly, more needs to be done in New York and throughout the Northeast, and our leaders in Washington must take greater measures to protect the environment from the ravages of greed and neglect. Indeed, we also need to find cooperative solutions internationally, because our environmental concerns transcend national borders.

Mr. Farb's eloquent photographs, and the work of present-day environmentalists, will impress upon citizens everywhere the need to make sensible accommodations with nature. Despite our technological proficiency, we are still dependent on an ecosystem that is as fragile as it is interconnected. We are all part of this "great chain of being," inheriting the legacy of those who preserved this earth before us. If we wish to safeguard our bountiful world for the future, we must balance more intelligently development with conservation, approaching the environment with both reason and humility, with wonder and reverence. We are grateful to Mr. Farb for helping us to do that.

ALBANY, NEW YORK
OCTOBER 1988

CONTENTS

MORNING VIEWS

INTIMATE VIEWS

MOUNTAIN VIEWS

AUSABLE VIEWS

MORNING VIEWS

FROM
A Letter

Scenery seems to wear in one's consciousness better than any other element in life . . . I have often been surprised to find what a predominant part in my own spiritual experience it has played, and how it stands out as almost the only thing the memory of which I should like to carry over with me beyond the veil, unamended and unaltered.

William James

WHITEFACE FROM CONNERY POND #1

FIRST SUNLIGHT REACHING CONNERY POND

WHITEFACE FROM CONNERY POND #3

WHITEFACE FROM CONNERY POND #4

AUSABLE VALLEY SUNRISE

WHITEFACE FROM CONNERY POND #2

FROM
My Adirondack Pipe

The silence and the solitude are delicious.

W.S.K.

UPPER CASCADE LAKE #1

20

LOWER CASCADE LAKE #1

21

LOWER CASCADE LAKE #2

SOUTH POND

BEAVER RIVER STILLWATER

LAKE LILA OUTLET

26

SALMON RIVER FLOW

INTIMATE VIEWS

FROM
Letters from the Backwoods

The still small voice of nature is more impressive than her loudest thunder.

Reverend J.T. Healy

DETAIL, DEW ON FUNGUS

DEW ON FUNGUS

PINCUSHION

32

RUSSIAN LAKE

MOOSE POND

ROOTS OF BLOWN-DOWN TREE

WOLFJAW BROOK

SENTINEL MOUNTAIN WOODS

LAKE LILA SHORELINE

BOUQUET RIVER VIEW #1

BIRCH #1

HEART LAKE #1

NEAR THE CROWS

NEAR FLOODWOOD POND

PHELPS MOUNTAIN WOODS

SHAD BUSH

BUNCHBERRY

MOUNTAIN VIEWS

The Land of Unloving

All men are pioneers inside their hearts,

They are forever seeking wilderness,

They are dreaming of lands

Uncivilized that sprawl

Unfound, or unimagined or forgot.

Lionel Wiggam

HEART LAKE #2

LAKE TEAR OF THE CLOUDS

MARCY AND THE GREAT RANGE

ALGONQUIN FROM PLAINS OF ABRAHAM

LOWER AUSABLE LAKE

CHAPEL POND #1

ELK LAKE #1, MORNING

ELK LAKE #2, STORM

UPPER AUSABLE LAKE #2

UPPER AUSABLE LAKE #3

ELK LAKE #3, EVENING

UPPER AUSABLE LAKE #1, ALLEN MOUNTAIN

UPPER AUSABLE LAKE #4, HAYSTACK MOUNTAIN

UPPER AUSABLE LAKE #5, GOTHICS

UPPER AUSABLE LAKE #6, GOTHICS

BASIN, ARMSTRONG, GOTHICS FROM HAYSTACK

The photographs in this section were made along the Ausable River, from its highest source on the north face of the Gothics to its end at Lake Champlain. The views are arranged according to elevation, skipping from tributary to tributary and from branch to branch of this Adirondack river.

AUSABLE VIEWS

FROM
The Rumination of Rivers

I fall asleep meditating rivers—

their flows, that gravity desires

their deep waters, determines their pull . . .

I think of slowness, patience, indifference

to time, their endurance as, almost lost

at the bottom of sculptured ruins worn and dug

as canyons, their flow goes on, their intention still

the same as though never was ever enough, though it is.

And my mind meanders in grassy, flatter lands;

in barely perceptible flow, I fall asleep.

William Bronk

74

OREBED BROOK

THE SLIDE ON OREBED BROOK

JOHNS BROOK

CLIFFORD BROOK

RAINBOW FALLS #1

RAINBOW FALLS #2

HULLS BROOK BASIN FLUME #1

HULLS BROOK BASIN FLUME #2

84

EAST BRANCH NEAR KEENE VALLEY

NICHOLS BROOK

FROM
The Changes

And there is weather here, and seasons, so that hour
by hour, month to month, it seems it could be
almost only by our own not moving that this
air-moved, light-moved, restless place
could be called, as we did call it, the same place.

William Bronk

STYLES BROOK FALLS #2

STYLES BROOK FALLS #3

EAST BRANCH FLUME

EAST BRANCH VIEW #1

FROM
White Lake

Amid this scene of light and gloom,
Nature with art links hand in hand,
Thick woods beside soft rural bloom,
As by a seer's command.

A.B. Street

RIVER BOTTOM, EAST BRANCH

EAST BRANCH VIEW #2

EAST BRANCH VIEW #3

EAST BRANCH VIEW #4

WEST BRANCH

EAST BRANCH VIEW #5

EAST BRANCH VIEW #6

EAST BRANCH VIEW #7

EAST BRANCH VIEW #8

AUSABLE CHASM

WINTER VIEWS

FROM
A Bright Day in December

So much light in what we call the dark
of the year, a flashing and glittering of light—
it quivers, it flaps in our face like slaps of wind.

William Bronk

WHITEFACE MOUNTAIN SUMMIT

CASCADE MOUNTAIN SUMMIT

PORTER AND THE RANGE

OLD MILITARY ROAD TRAIL

WAINWRIGHT MOUNTAIN

BOUQUET RIVER VIEW #2

BOUQUET RIVER VIEW #3

The Adirondacs, A Journal

As water poured through hollows of the hills

To feed this wealth of lakes and rivulets,

So Nature shed all beauty lavishly

From her redundant horn.

Ralph Waldo Emerson

SPLIT ROCK FALLS

DETAIL, SPLIT ROCK FALLS

UNTITLED

NEW SNOW #1

NEW SNOW #2

NEW SNOW #3

124

COREYS ROAD #1

COREYS ROAD #2

BEAVER MEADOW #1

BEAVER MEADOW #2

MONDRIAN'S TREE

WETLAND VIEWS

The Story that the Keg Told Me

In such a place the sense of time passes from you,
and the sense of eternity is experienced.

William H. Murray

BIG BROOK

RAQUETTE RIVER

TUPPER LAKE SWAMP

UNTITLED

SARANAC RIVER

CHUBB RIVER

137

AVALANCHE PASS, BEAVER POND

LODO POND

BROWN'S TRACT INLET

PANTHER MOUNTAIN SWAMP #1

PANTHER MOUNTAIN SWAMP #2

ST. REGIS RIVER VEGETATION #1

ST. REGIS RIVER VEGETATION #2

DROUGHT-STRICKEN WETLANDS

In late September and early October 1987, one of the earliest and heaviest snows fell over New England. Old-timers said it was a once-in-a-century occurrence.

AUTUMN SNOW

FROM
Recompense

Chilly blow the north winds o'er

Forests lone and meadows sere;

Autumn has come, and the earth once more

Feels the weight of the aged year.

Arthur E. Smith

BAXTER AND ASTERS

153

SNOW ON RIVER

CHAPEL POND #2

MARCY

COLDEN AND ALGONQUIN

FROM
Woods & Waters

The arcades of the forest would glow, darken,
be masked in the shower, and flash again into gold.

A. B. Street

UPPER CASCADE LAKE #2

DETAIL, UPPER CASCADE LAKE #2

CHAPEL POND #3

NOONMARK

CHAPEL POND #4

CHAPEL POND #5

ROARING BROOK FALLS

ACKNOWLEDGMENTS

Many people lent a hand on the trails; some carried heavy photographic equipment, others were just there, offering encouragement and friendship. One couple, in fact, rescued me when I was two miles into the woods on the frozen day when I dislocated my shoulder.

For their support and input, I thank: Jeanne Ashworth, Allison Bell, Dan Bross, Dave Brown, Jennifer Deming, Dave Doeman, Susy Doolittle, Esme Farb, Fred Foster, King T. Fok, Robert Janjigian, Carol Kennedy, Anne Lacy, Vern and Winnie Lamb, Philippe Laumont, Rich McDonald, Amanda Means, Ann and Bill Messnard, Frank Murray, Ian O'Brien, June O'Neill, Ben Pelaez, Chris Pell, Robin Pell, Midge Saber, Ruth Sergel, Catherine Syrbe, Carter and Julia Walker, and the Clarkson Adirondack Conference Lodge.

Special thanks go to Nai Chang for his sympathetic eye and creative contributions.

CREDITS

The thoughts on the Adirondacks that appear in this book are excerpted from the sources cited below. Numbers in parentheses indicate pages on which the contributions appear.

"An Adirondack Friendship: Letters of William James," by Josephine Goldmark. Copyright © 1934 Josephine Goldmark, as published in *The Atlantic Monthly,* September 1934 (10).

My Adirondack Pipe: Memories of a pleasant month spent in the Adirondacks by W.S.K. Printed for private circulation, New York: Press of W.R. Jenkins, 1887, p. 70. Reprinted courtesy of The Arents Collection, The New York Public Library, Astor, Lenox and Tilden Foundations (18).

Letters from the Backwoods by Reverend J.T. Healy, New York: John S. Taylor, Publisher, 1850, p. 70 (28).

"All Men Are Pioneers," from *The Land of Unloving* by Lionel Wiggam. Copyright © 1936, 1961, 1964 by Lionel Wiggam. Reprinted with permission of Macmillan Publishing Company (48).

"The Rumination of Rivers," from *Life Supports* by William Bronk, Copyright © 1982 by William Bronk. Published by North Point Press and reprinted by permission (72).

"The Changes," from *Life Supports* by William Bronk, Copyright © 1982 by William Bronk. Published by North Point Press and reprinted by permission (86).

"White Lake," by A.B. Street, from *The New York Book of Poetry,* New York: G. Dearborn, Publisher, 1837. Reprinted courtesy of The Arents Collection, The New York Public Library, Astor, Lenox and Tilden Foundations (92).

"A Bright Day in December," from *Life Supports* by William Bronk, Copyright © 1982 by William Bronk. Published by North Point Press and reprinted by permission. (106).

"The Adirondacs, A Journal," 1858, by Ralph Waldo Emerson, from *The Complete Works of Ralph Waldo Emerson, Poems* Volume 9, New York: Houghton Mifflin & Company, 1904, p. 187 (114)

"The Story That The Keg Told Me," from *Adirondack Tales* by William Henry Murray, Boston: Golden Publishing, 1877, p. 9 (130).

"Recompense," from *Rural Legends and Lyrics* by Arthur E. Smith, New York: John B. Alden Publishers, 1892 (152).

Woods & Waters or The Saranac & Racket by A.B. Street, New York: M. Doolady Publishers, 1860. Reprinted by Harbor Hill Books, 1976, p. 199. (158).